# SPOOKS' SURPRISE

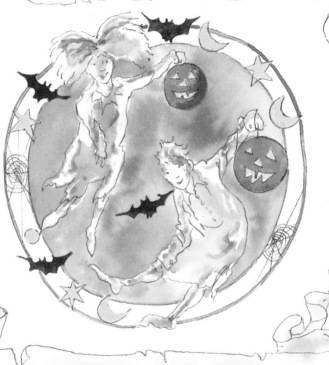

Karen Dolby

Illustrated by Alan Marks

Designed by I

500766981

# Contents

# About this Book

This book is about a creepy, old house called Spook Hall. Some people say the house is haunted. You can find out more by turning the page . . .

There are puzzles along the way. See if you can solve them.

Keep your eyes open for clues. If you get stuck, there are answers on pages 31 and 32.

# Spook Hall

In the moonlight, the house looks dark and eerie. It is easy to see why people are frightened of Spook Hall. And, in fact, the house IS haunted by a family of ghosts called the Spookenshivers, or Spooks for short ~ Sam and Sorrel, Ma, Pa and Baby, Grandpa and Grandma and Aunt Serena.

**Can you find seven Spooks? (You can't see Baby. She is asleep inside.)**

# The Spookenshivers

There have been Spookenshivers at Spook Hall for centuries and they love their home. There was a time when they had to share it with some unfriendly humans who tried to chase the ghosts away. But nobody has lived at the Hall for a very long time now and that is just the way the Spooks like it.

*Sir Lancelot Lander ghost hunting*

Ma and Sorrel cook up some spooky soup.

Sam, Sorrel, Ma, Pa and Baby live in the main part of the house. Grandpa and Grandma live in the East Turret and Aunt Serena is usually in the belfry. Here are some pictures from their family album.

Pa and Sam check the creeping vine.

Grandma knits (and knits) a scarf.

Grandpa takes a rooftop stroll.

Aunt Serena hanging around with her pet bats.

Sam has a small brown fruit bat called Bertie which his Aunt gave him for his birthday. Bertie likes playing games and hiding.

**Can you spot Bertie hiding in one of the pictures?**

# Gloomy Grandpa

One day, Sorrel was floating around with nothing much to do when she heard a loud, rattling sound. A cloud of soot whooshed out from the fireplace and there was a long moaning sigh. The dust settled and Sorrel saw . . .

"Grandpa!"

He was sitting on the hearth looking grubby and sorry for himself. "Oh dear . . . Oh dear," he exclaimed.

What had upset Grandpa? When Sorrel looked outside, she thought she knew.

**Do you know?**

"If someone buys the Hall, we'll have people living here and we'll have to find a new home," Grandpa sighed. "I'm too old to start haunting and sharing our house with humans again. I remember the days when the whole place rattled, howled, clanked and groaned with ghosts. Phantoms came from far and wide and no humans came near."

# Sorrel's Plan

Grandpa floated away looking glum but Sorrel had an idea.

"We can't stop the Hall being sold," she explained to Sam. "But I know how we can cheer up Grandpa. It's his birthday next Friday. Let's invite all his friends to a surprise party and give Grandpa a birthday to remember."

They spent the rest of the day in the library writing invitations.

## GRANDPA SPOOKENSHIVERS BIRTHDAY BALL

A ghoulish, ghostly, surprise ball is to be held by the Spookenshivers of Spook Hall.

The party's on Friday and starts at 8. Wear something haunting for this Spooky date.

   This left just one problem ~ how to deliver the invitations. There was a ghostly post office but as ghosts sent so many letters and lived in such unusual, far-flung places, the letter could take weeks to arrive.

   "The only way to be sure everyone has their invitation in time is to deliver them ourselves. We can find out where Grandpa's friends live from his haunted address book," said Sam. "It's blue with a red ribbon."

**Can you spot Grandpa's book?**

# Sam and Sorrel Set off

Early next morning, the two young Spooks flew off with Grandpa's book, a stack of invitations and a list of ghostly guests. The first ghost on their list was the one who lived farthest away. He was a Roman Centurion called Paulus and he lived in a Roman ruin.

When they reached the ruins, they sat down on an ancient arch and looked at Grandpa's book. They had to match Grandpa's map to the scene in front of them.

"The blue arrow points to where Paulus lives," said Sam.

**Can you work out where Paulus lives?**

# The Haunted Forest

Can I bring Wolfgang?

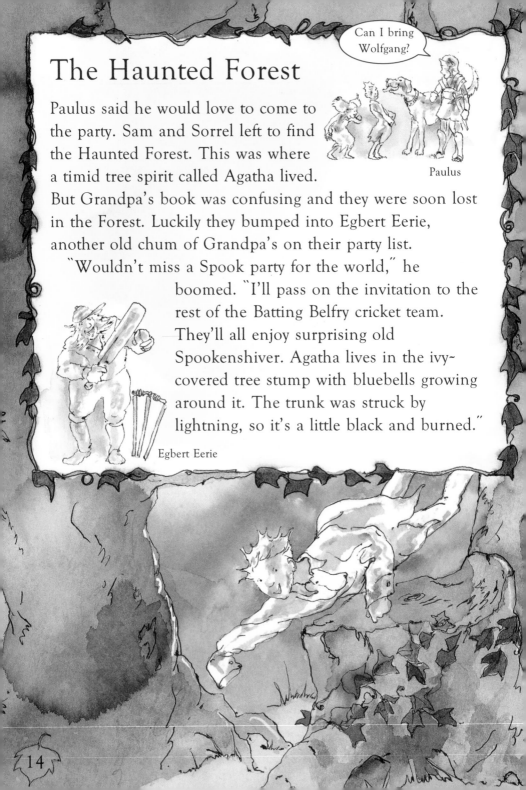

Paulus said he would love to come to
the party. Sam and Sorrel left to find
the Haunted Forest. This was where
a timid tree spirit called Agatha lived.

Paulus

But Grandpa's book was confusing and they were soon lost
in the Forest. Luckily they bumped into Egbert Eerie,
another old chum of Grandpa's on their party list.

"Wouldn't miss a Spook party for the world," he
boomed. "I'll pass on the invitation to the
rest of the Batting Belfry cricket team.
They'll all enjoy surprising old
Spookenshiver. Agatha lives in the ivy~
covered tree stump with bluebells growing
around it. The trunk was struck by
lightning, so it's a little black and burned."

Egbert Eerie

Can you see which tree
stump Agatha lives in?

# Creepy Castle

At first Agatha would not
come outside. But when she
heard about Grandpa's
surprise party, an arm shot
out from the tree trunk and
grabbed the invitation.

"O.K. I'll be there," she called.

In the distance, Sam and Sorrel could see the towers
and turrets of Creepy Castle, the home of Grandpa's
old friends the Jesters. The front door was locked but as
they were Spooks, Sam and Sorrel were able to find
other ways in.

CREEPY CASTLE

"Ha ha ha haaaa," ghostly laughter echoed through the castle. "Whoo hoo hoo are you hoo hoo?" a soft voice asked.

When Sorrel explained, the voice answered, "You will have to come and find usssss."

Sam remembered Grandpa saying that the Jesters of Creepy Castle were always playing tricks. There was no choice but to join in the ghostly game of hide-and-seek.

**Can you find five hidden ghosts?**

# Dank, Dark Dungeon

The playful ghosts all said they would come to the party.

"Don't forget Cecil. He's the gloomy ghoul in the dungeon," one called, as Sam and Sorrel were about to leave. They slid down slimy stone steps to the dankest, darkest depths of the castle.

At first it was hard to see but they soon spotted Cecil behind a pillar looking miserable.

"We've come to invite you to Grandpa's surprise party,"
said Sam. "What's the matter?"

"I've lost my ball and chain," groaned Cecil. "I can't go
anywhere without them."

"We'll help you to look for them," said Sorrel, beginning
the hunt.

**Can you find Cecil's ball and chain?**

# Walter's Puzzling Path

They left Cecil clanking his ball and chain around the cellar and flew out to the lake. A rocky path led from the shore to a cave. This was the home of Walter, a water ghost. Sorrel and Sam were simply about to fly over the lake when a grouchy voice called out, "Find your way across the stones, otherwise I will NOT talk to you! But watch out for lurking creatures and no cheating!"

**Can you find a path across the lake to Walter?**

# A Ghostly Trail

Walter was not at all grouchy when Sam and Sorrel invited him to the party. He even told them which way to go to Forest Farm, their next stop. This was where Grandpa's great pal, Cuthbert, kept his coach and horses.

There was no sign of Cuthbert at the farm. But a real, live, small boy soon hurried across to them.

"Aren't you scared of us?" Sorrel said, surprised.

"Why should I be?" said the boy. "I like ghosts. If you're looking for Cuthbert, you should follow his horse's hoofprints."

Sure enough, there WERE hoofprints glowing white in the sunshine. Sorrel quickly saw where Cuthbert and his horses must be.

**Can you see where the hoofprints lead?**

# The Rattling Bones Studio

Now all the guests were invited,
they needed music for the party. Sorrel
and Sam decided to call at the Rattling Bones Studio. Sorrel
could hear a terrible noise as she opened the door. Inside
she found the six members of the Ghoulish Groovers group
squabbling loudly. Gary Groover explained the problem.

"All our instruments have been lost or mixed up.
Ned has his drums but no drumsticks. Oliver has a bow
but no violin. Millie has her stool, but no piano and I've
lost my saxophone," Gary said. "Gloria has her guitar
and Kate sings but they can't find their music."

Sam and Sorrel were sure they could help.

**Can you spot the musical instruments and music for the
group to play?**

# Party Store

The Ghoulish Groovers promised to arrive on time for Grandpa's surprise party. Sam heard them begin to play as he closed the door.

"All we have to do now is find the Party Store for some special ghostly party decorations," said Sorrel. "What shall we buy?"

As they floated along, the two young Spooks thought about what they should choose.

"We need lightning flashes, party mist, green slime and shivers, please," Sorrel told the storekeeper.

"And we also want streamers, pumpkin lanterns and glowing skulls," added Sam, as a shiver ran over his foot.

**Can you spot everything on their party list?**

# Surprise Party

On Grandpa's birthday, Grandma took a grumpy Grandpa out for the day so Ma, Pa, Aunt Serena, Sam and Sorrel could make sure Spook Hall looked its spooky best for his surprise party. At last all was ready ~ the Spooks were wearing their party clothes, the group was ready to play and the guests had arrived. Everything was waiting for Grandpa.

All was silent, the lights were dimmed, everyone was hidden. Grandpa opened the door and leaped back in amazement as the whole house exploded into light and sound in front of him. Thunder cracked and lightning lit up the sky. The Ghoulish Groovers struck up a tune and Grandpa's ghostly chums appeared everywhere chorusing, "SURPRISE! Happy birthday!"

**Can you spot all the ghosts that Sam and Sorrel invited?**

# Spooks' Surprise

"It's the best birthday I've ever had. Thank you!" exclaimed Grandpa, happily.

The surprise party was wonderful and everyone was having fun. But there was another surprise in store.

Sorrel pointed at the window. "Look," she exclaimed. Two terrified people were being chased away from Spook Hall. "I don't think anyone will want to buy our house for a very long time to come. Our Spooks' Surprise couldn't have turned out better."

# Answers

## Pages 4-5

You can see the seven Spooks circled in this picture.

## Pages 6-7

Bertie is hiding here among the vine leaves.

## Pages 8-9

Grandpa is upset because he has seen a real person outside and a FOR SALE sign.

## Pages 10-11

Grandpa's address book is circled here. It is the only blue book with a red ribbon.

## Pages 12-13

Paulus lives here.

## Pages 14-15

Agatha lives in this tree trunk. It is the only stump that is ivy-covered and blackened with bluebells growing around it.

## Pages 16-17
The five hidden ghosts are circled here.

## Pages 18-19
Here are Cecil's ball and chain.

## Pages 20-21
The path across to Walter is marked in black.

## Pages 22-23
The hoofprints lead to this barn.

## Pages 24-25
The missing instruments and music are circled here.

## Pages 26-27

Glowing skulls · Green slime · Pumpkin lanterns · Streamers · Lightning flashes · Mist · Shivers

## Pages 28-29

Cuthbert · Egbert Eerie · Paulus · Walter · Cecil · Agatha · Creepy Castle Ghosts · The Ghoulish Groovers

This edition first published in 2002 by Usborne Publishing Ltd., Usborne House, 83-85 Saffron Hill, London EC1N 8RT, England. www.usborne.com Copyright © 2002, 1995 Usborne Publishing Ltd. The name Usborne and the devices 🔔 🌐 are Trade Marks of Usborne Publishing Ltd. All rights reserved.